BIGGEST NAMES IN SPORTS

JOE BURROW

by Harold P. Cain

FOOTBALL STAR

FOCUS READERS®

NAVIGATOR

WWW.FOCUSREADERS.COM

Focus Readers is distributed by North Star Editions:
sales@northstareditions.com | 888-417-0195

Produced for Focus Readers by Red Line Editorial.

Photographs ©: Robin Alam/Icon Sportswire/AP Images, cover, 1; Scott Winters/Icon Sportswire/AP Images, 4–5, 7; Charlie Riedel/AP Images, 9; Scott W. Grau/Icon Sportswire/AP Images, 10–11; JP Waldron/Cal Sport Media/AP Images, 13; Jonathan Mailhes/Cal Sport Media/ZUMA Wire/AP Images, 15; Aaron Doster/AP Images, 16–17; Aaron M. Sprecher/AP Images, 19; Ian Johnson/Icon Sportswire/AP Images, 21; Jeff Dean/AP Images, 22–23; Emilee Chinn/AP Images, 25; Elaine Thompson/AP Images, 27; Red Line Editorial, 29

Library of Congress Cataloging-in-Publication Data
Library of Congress Cataloging-in-Publication Data is available on the Library of Congress website.

ISBN
978-1-63739-438-0 (hardcover)
978-1-63739-439-7 (paperback)
978-1-63739-441-0 (ebook pdf)
978-1-63739-440-3 (hosted ebook)

Printed in the United States of America
Mankato, MN
082022

ABOUT THE AUTHOR

Harold P. Cain is a retired English teacher and lifelong sports fan originally from Rockford, Illinois. He and his wife now live in Cathedral City, California, where they enjoy hiking, golf, and spending time with their daughter and three grandchildren in Los Angeles.

TABLE OF CONTENTS

CHAPTER 1

COMEBACK KID

Cincinnati Bengals fans had waited more than 30 years for this game. Their team was just one win away from the Super Bowl. However, the 2021 season seemed to be slipping away. Cincinnati had fallen behind 21–3 to the Kansas City Chiefs. Bengals quarterback Joe Burrow didn't panic. He got to work.

Joe Burrow attempts a pass during the conference championship game against the Kansas City Chiefs.

Cincinnati had a great offense. Burrow knew he could rely on star receivers Ja'Marr Chase and Tee Higgins. He also had plenty of other weapons. Late in the first half, Burrow tossed a short pass to running back Samaje Perine. Perine ran 41 yards to score a touchdown. The Bengals went into halftime down by 11 points.

In the third quarter, Burrow led his team to a field goal. Now the Bengals trailed by only eight. Later in the third, the Bengals defense made an **interception**. That put Burrow and the offense in great field position. Burrow found Chase for a two-yard touchdown. Then he connected

Burrow looks for a receiver as a Chiefs defender chases him.

with Trent Taylor to make the two-point conversion. The game was now tied at 21.

In the fourth quarter, Burrow led the Bengals to another field goal. That put Cincinnati on top 24–21. However, the Chiefs scored a field goal as time expired. The game was heading to overtime.

Kansas City got the ball first. But the Bengals defense came up big again, forcing another interception. Burrow took advantage of the opportunity. He drove his team all the way to the 13-yard line. A short field goal would win the game.

Bengals kicker Evan McPherson sent the ball through the uprights. The

BEST OF THE BEST

Joe Burrow was the No. 1 overall pick in the 2020 National Football League (NFL) **Draft**. Fans always expect big things from the top pick. And Burrow didn't disappoint. He was the first No. 1 overall pick to lead his team to the Super Bowl in just two seasons.

Bengals defensive tackle Tyler Shelvin lifts Burrow to celebrate their conference championship.

Bengals were going to the Super Bowl for the first time since 1988. Burrow had led the biggest **comeback** in **conference** championship history.

CHAPTER 2

MR. FOOTBALL

Joe Burrow was born in Ames, Iowa, on December 10, 1996. As a kid, football shaped Joe's life. In fact, football is the reason he was born in Iowa. Joe's father, Jim, was a coach at Iowa State University. Jim passed his love of the sport to Joe.

Jim's coaching career took the family to Nebraska, North Dakota, and finally Ohio.

Joe Burrow leads the Athens High School offense in 2014.

Jim became the defensive **coordinator** at Ohio University in Athens. That was where Joe went to high school. Before Joe, Athens High School had never won a playoff game. With Joe, the team won seven. In 2014, he was named the best high school football player in Ohio.

HOMETOWN HERO

Joe Burrow was the greatest football player in Athens High School history. In 2019, the school honored him by renaming its field Joe Burrow Stadium. When Joe attended Athens, that part of Ohio didn't have many Bengals fans. But once he reached the NFL, more people started cheering for the Bengals. They wanted to support their hometown hero.

Burrow runs the ball during a 2016 game between Ohio State and Bowling Green.

Several big colleges wanted Burrow to play for them. He decided to stay near home and attended Ohio State University. However, the Buckeyes already had several talented quarterbacks. As a result,

Burrow didn't get much playing time. After three years as a backup, Burrow wanted a chance to play. He transferred to Louisiana State University (LSU) before the 2018 season.

Burrow earned the starting quarterback job right away at LSU. He led the Tigers to a win in the Fiesta Bowl. And he was just getting started. In 2019, Burrow won the Heisman Trophy. That award is given to the best player in college football.

The Tigers were the top seed in the College Football Playoff. In the semifinal, Burrow threw for seven touchdowns and ran for another. The Tigers then defeated Clemson to win the national title.

Burrow scores a touchdown for LSU in the national championship game.

Burrow passed for 463 yards and five touchdowns in the game. That gave him 60 passing touchdowns for the season, which was an all-time record. There was no doubt that Burrow would be a top pick in that year's NFL Draft.

CHAPTER 3

BACK TO OHIO

The 2019 season was a rough one for the Cincinnati Bengals. They finished 2–14. However, the Bengals' awful record meant they got the first draft pick. And that meant Joe Burrow was coming home to Ohio.

Bengals fans expected big things from Burrow. As a **rookie** in 2020, he earned

Burrow competes against the Los Angeles Chargers in his first game as a pro.

the chance to start right away. The Bengals weren't a good team. Even so, Burrow had some weapons on offense. A. J. Green was the team's star receiver. Joe Mixon was a talented running back.

Still, the Bengals leaned heavily on their young quarterback. In his second game, Burrow set a rookie record with 37 pass completions. However, it wasn't enough to get a win. Cincinnati lost a close one to the Cleveland Browns.

Burrow's first win came two weeks later. He passed for 300 yards against the Jacksonville Jaguars. That was his third week in a row with 300 yards or more. It was another rookie record.

Burrow fires a pass against the Cleveland Browns in Week 2 of the 2020 season.

Burrow had his share of struggles, too. In Weeks 5 and 6, he didn't throw any touchdown passes. However, Burrow bounced back in Week 7. He recorded his first 400-yard game.

After eight games, Burrow had completed 221 passes. That was the most ever for a quarterback in the first eight games of his career. More importantly, Burrow led the Bengals to another win in Week 8.

FEEDING THE HUNGRY

In 2019, Burrow used his Heisman Trophy speech to call out a serious problem. Many people in his Ohio hometown didn't have enough food to eat. In the weeks that followed, people began donating money to a food pantry. That led to the creation of the Joe Burrow Hunger Relief Fund. By 2022, the fund had raised $1.5 million. It helped feed hungry people in Ohio.

Burrow leads Cincinnati to a victory over the Tennessee Titans in 2020.

Unfortunately, Burrow's season was cut short in Week 11. He suffered a serious knee injury during a game against Washington. That kept Burrow on the sidelines for the rest of the year. Bengals fans could only hope that he would be healthy in time for the 2021 season.

CHAPTER 4

SUPER SEASON

Bengals fans were thrilled when the 2021 season began. Joe Burrow had recovered from last season's injury. Cincinnati's offense was also ready to take a big step forward. Wide receivers Ja'Marr Chase, Tee Higgins, and Tyler Boyd formed a trio of targets for Burrow.

A healthy Joe Burrow plays in Week 1 of the 2021 season.

The team seemed to get better as the year went on. The Bengals were chasing a playoff spot. They also had a shot at the division title. In Week 16, Burrow set a team record with 525 passing yards. The win put Cincinnati in first place.

The next week, Burrow recorded 446 passing yards against the Kansas City Chiefs. The Bengals won the game. That clinched the division title. Burrow finished the season with 4,611 passing yards and 34 touchdowns. Both were team records.

Cincinnati hadn't won a playoff game since the 1990 season. Burrow was determined to end that streak. In the first round, he threw two touchdown passes.

Burrow calls a play against the Kansas City Chiefs.

That helped the Bengals defeat the Las Vegas Raiders.

The Tennessee Titans were up next. Burrow was **sacked** nine times in the game. Even so, he threw for 348 yards. He led his team to an amazing last-second victory. The following week, Cincinnati faced the Kansas City Chiefs. Burrow's historic comeback sent the Bengals to their first Super Bowl in decades.

The Bengals took on the Los Angeles Rams in the big game. Los Angeles led 13–10 at halftime. But in the second half, Burrow came out hot. He tossed a 75-yard touchdown to Higgins just 12 seconds

JOE WHO?

During the 2021 season, Burrow became a beloved star in Cincinnati. Fans enjoyed coming up with all sorts of nicknames for him. One was "Joey Franchise." That name showed how much he meant to the Bengals team. Another was "Joe Cool." That was for his calm presence on the field.

Burrow threw for 263 yards and one touchdown in the Super Bowl.

into the third quarter. Unfortunately for Bengals fans, it wasn't enough. The Rams ended up winning 23–20.

The loss was tough. Still, Burrow had done what many Bengals fans thought was impossible. He'd brought the team back to the Super Bowl. Fans couldn't wait to see what he would do next.

JOE BURROW

- Height: 6 feet 4 inches (193 cm)
- Weight: 221 pounds (100 kg)
- Birth date: December 10, 1996
- Birthplace: Ames, Iowa
- High school: Athens High School (Athens, Ohio)
- College: Ohio State University (Columbus, Ohio) (2015–17); Louisiana State University (Baton Rouge, Louisiana) (2018–19)
- NFL team: Cincinnati Bengals (2020–)
- Major awards: Heisman Trophy (2019); College Football Playoff champion (2019); NFL Comeback Player of the Year (2021)

Columbus

Ames

Athens

Cincinnati

Baton Rouge

FOCUS ON
JOE BURROW

Write your answers on a separate piece of paper.

1. Write a sentence that describes the main idea of Chapter 2.

2. Do you think Burrow would have won the Rookie of the Year Award in 2020 if he hadn't gotten hurt? Why or why not?

3. In the 2021 season, which team did the Bengals beat in the first round of the playoffs?

    A. Las Vegas Raiders
    B. Tennessee Titans
    C. Los Angeles Rams

4. Why did Burrow leave Ohio State after three seasons?

    A. He was tired of living so close to his hometown.
    B. He didn't want to be a backup anymore.
    C. He was ready to start his career in the NFL.

Answer key on page 32.

GLOSSARY

comeback
A situation where a team is losing but ends up winning the game.

conference
A group of teams within a league.

coordinator
A coach who runs either the offense or defense.

draft
A system that allows teams to acquire new players coming into a league.

interception
A play in which the defense catches a pass, gaining possession of the ball.

rookie
A professional athlete in his or her first year.

sacked
Tackled the quarterback behind the line of scrimmage before he could pass the ball.

TO LEARN MORE

BOOKS

Anderson, Josh. *Cincinnati Bengals*. Mankato, MN: The Child's World, 2022.

Coleman, Ted. *Cincinnati Bengals All-Time Greats*. Lake Elmo, MN: Press Room Editions, 2022.

Fishman, Jon M. *Joe Burrow*. Minneapolis: Lerner Publications, 2022.

NOTE TO EDUCATORS

Visit **www.focusreaders.com** to find lesson plans, activities, links, and other resources related to this title.

INDEX

Answer Key: 1. Answers will vary; **2.** Answers will vary; **3.** A; **4.** B